WHAT AM I?

Fierce, Strong, and Snappy

WHAT AM I?

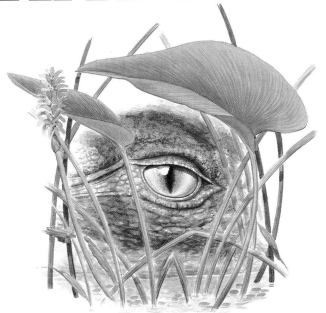

By Moira Butterfield
Illustrated by Wayne Ford

RSVP

RAINTREE
STECK-VAUGHN
P U B L I S H E R S
The Steck-Vaughn Company

Austin, Texas

Published by Raintree Steck-Vaughn Publishers, an imprint of Steck-Vaughn Company.

Editors: Stephanie Bellwood, Heather Luff
Project Manager: Joyce Spicer
Designer: Helen James
Illustrator: Wayne Ford / Wildlife Art Agency
Consultant: Andrew Branson

Library of Congress Cataloging-in-Publication Data

Butterfield, Moira, 1961-
    Fierce, Strong, and Snappy/by Moira Butterfield;
illustrated by Wayne Ford.
        p.   cm. — (What Am I?)
    Summary: Presents the life of an alligator, in the form of a riddle.
    ISBN 0-8172-4588-X (hardcover)
    ISBN 0-8172-7225-9 (softcover)
    1. American alligator — Juvenile literature.
[1. Alligators.   2. Riddles.]   I. Ford, Wayne, ill.   II. Title.
III. Seires.
Ol666.C925B877   1998
597.98—dc21   96-54493
                                        CIP   AC

Printed in Hong Kong

3 4 5 6 7 8 9 0 WO 03 02 01

My tail is long.
My skin is rough.
It's scaly, thick, and very tough.
When my mouth is open wide,
you will see my big, sharp teeth inside!

What am I?

Here is my eye.

At night I float
in my watery
home. My eyes
shine in the
silver moonlight.

I look for animals
to gobble up. If
that tasty turtle
comes near me,
I will pounce on it.

7

Here is my skin.

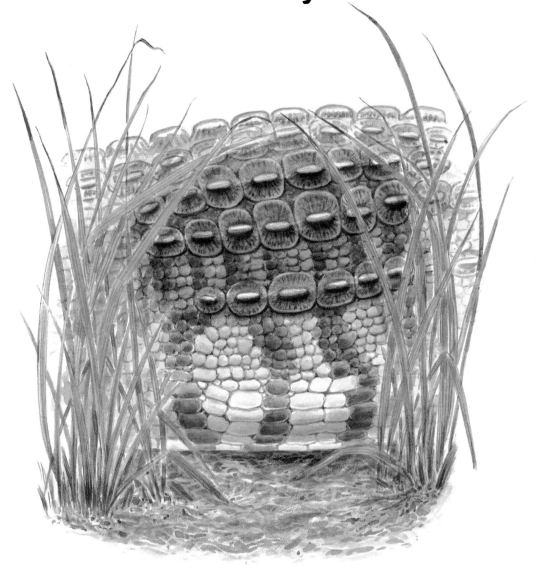

My skin is very
thick to protect me
from getting hurt.
Look how rough
and scaly it is.

When I float in
the water, I look
just like a tree log.
Can you find me
in this swamp?

Here is my nose.

It is called a snout,
and it has two big
nostrils on top.
They close when
I swim under water.

Sometimes I crawl
onto land. I use
my snout to smell
food. This raccoon
looks good to eat.

11

Here is my back.

In warm weather
I sunbathe by the
water. I love to feel
the hot sun shining
on my back.

I am long, but not
tall. My belly drags
along the ground
and makes a
muddy trail.

13

Here is my foot.

My feet help me
to swim well. They
have sharp claws.
I use my claws to dig
a den by the water.

Sometimes the
swamp dries up.
I dig a water-filled
hole and stay safe
inside. What is
sharing my hole?

Here are my teeth.

I have eighty sharp
teeth to bite and
tear food. My jaw
is so strong that
I can crush a bone.

When I close my
mouth, my bottom
teeth are hidden.
This means that
I am not a crocodile.

Here is my tail.

I swish my tail and make a loud noise, like a lion's roar, to tell other animals where I am.

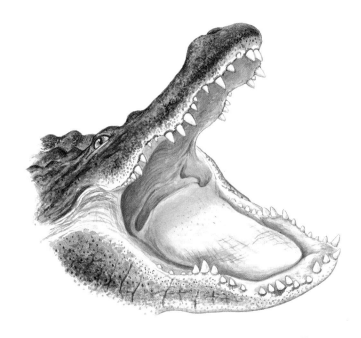

I open my mouth and...
bellow!
Have you guessed what I am?

I am an alligator.

Point to my ...

pointed teeth.

long tail.

sharp claws.

yellow eyes.

two nostrils.

rough skin.

I am called an
American alligator.

Here are my babies.

They are called hatchlings, and they hatch from eggs. I make a cozy nest for them.

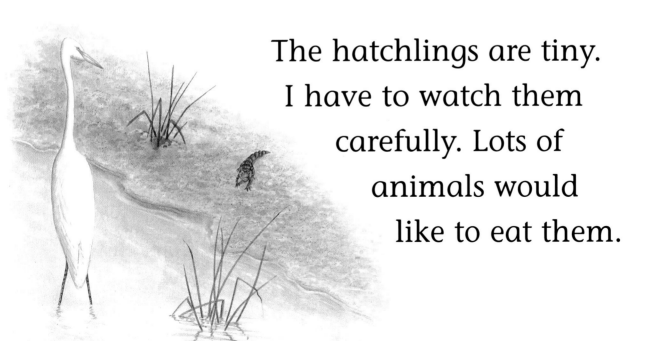

The hatchlings are tiny. I have to watch them carefully. Lots of animals would like to eat them.

Here is my home.

I live in swamps and lakes.

How many alligators can you see?
Can you find a cottonmouth snake, a bird
called a great white egret, and two raccoons?

Here is a map of the world.

I live in the southeastern part of North America. Where is it on the map?

North America

Can you point to the place where you live?

27

Can you answer these questions about me?

How many sharp
teeth do I have?

What is my skin like?

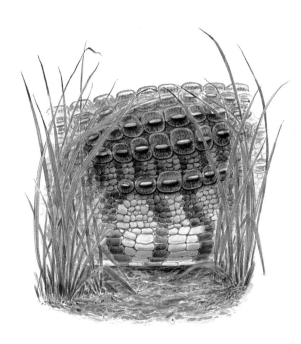

What is my
nose called?

Where do I live?

What are my
babies called?

What color
are my eyes?

How do I hunt
for my food?

Can you name
some animals
I like to eat?

Here are words to help you learn about me.

bellow The noise I make. It sounds like a lion roaring.

claws My sharp nails. I use them to dig my den in the ground.

den A cozy hole that I dig near the water's edge. I sleep here in winter.

hatchling The name for one of my babies when it has just hatched from its egg.

nostrils The two holes on top of my nose. I breathe through my nostrils just like you.

pounce To jump on something and grab it quickly. I catch my food this way.

scaly Dry and rough. My skin is scaly.

snout My nose. It is wide and it has two nostrils on the top.

swamp My watery, muddy home.

trail A muddy path I make when I crawl out of the water onto land.